The LaTeX Pocket Guide: Useful For Both Basic Understanding and Reference

Written By Richard Aragon

Introduction

Welcome to the exciting world of LaTeX! This comprehensive guide is designed to equip you with the knowledge and skills to harness the power of this versatile typesetting system. Whether you're a student preparing academic papers, a researcher writing reports, or a creative individual crafting beautiful documents, LaTeX offers a powerful tool for crafting high-quality, professional-looking outputs.

This book takes you on a journey from the basics of LaTeX syntax and commands to advanced topics like automation, scripting, and integration with other software. Through clear explanations, practical examples, and insightful tips, you will gain a strong foundation in LaTeX and unlock its full potential.

Here's what you can expect to find in this book:

- A comprehensive overview of LaTeX: Understand the core concepts, syntax, and structure of LaTeX documents.
- Detailed guidance on essential commands: Master the fundamental commands for formatting text, creating lists, inserting tables, and adding figures.
- Exploration of advanced features: Delve into macros, templates, packages, automation, and scripting to unleash the full power of LaTeX.
- Examples and exercises: Apply your newfound knowledge through practical examples and exercises, solidifying your understanding and building confidence.
- Tips and tricks: Discover valuable insights and best practices for efficient LaTeX workflow and document creation.
- Resources for further learning: Explore a wealth of online resources, tutorials, and communities to continue your LaTeX journey.

By the end of this book, you will be equipped to:

- Create professional-looking documents: Produce high-quality documents with consistent formatting, typography, and layout.
- Customize and personalize your documents: Adapt LaTeX to your specific needs and preferences through macros, packages, and templates.
- Automate repetitive tasks: Streamline your workflow by automating repetitive tasks with scripts and tools.
- Integrate with other software: Combine the power of LaTeX with other applications for enhanced functionality.
- Collaborate effectively: Share your LaTeX projects with others and work collaboratively on documents.
- Continue learning and expanding your skills: Use the resources provided to deepen your knowledge and stay updated with the latest LaTeX advancements.

So, embark on this exciting journey with us and discover the world of LaTeX. Let us guide you through the process of transforming your ideas into beautiful and professional documents.

Chapter 1: What is LaTeX?

Welcome to the exciting world of LaTeX! This chapter will introduce you to the fundamentals of this powerful typesetting system and explain why it is a valuable tool for students, researchers, writers, and professionals across various fields.

1.1 What is LaTeX?

LaTeX is a high-quality typesetting system designed for the creation of professional-looking documents. It is widely used in academia, scientific research, and various industries due to its ability to produce consistently formatted and aesthetically pleasing documents.

Unlike traditional word processors like Microsoft Word, which focus on the visual appearance of text while typing, LaTeX uses a markup language approach. This means that you write your document using plain text and specific commands to define the structure and formatting. This may seem less intuitive at first, but it offers several advantages, which we will discuss later in this chapter.

1.2 Advantages of using LaTeX

LaTeX provides several advantages over traditional word processors, including:

High-Quality Typesetting: LaTeX produces documents with superior typography compared to word processors. It automatically handles spacing, fonts, and layout, ensuring consistent and professional results.

Flexibility: LaTeX is highly customizable, allowing you to tailor the appearance of your document to specific needs. You can define custom layouts, fonts, styles, and even create your own macros for repetitive tasks.

Version Control: LaTeX documents are plain text files, making them easy to version control using tools like Git. This allows you to track changes and collaborate effectively with others.

Free and Open-Source: LaTeX is free and open-source software available on all major platforms. This makes it accessible to anyone without any licensing costs.

Focus on Content: Since LaTeX separates content from formatting, it allows you to focus on writing without worrying about constantly adjusting the visual appearance of your document.

Accessibility: LaTeX documents can be easily converted to various formats, including PDF, HTML, and ePub, ensuring accessibility for readers with different needs.

1.3 Disadvantages of using LaTeX

While LaTeX offers numerous advantages, it also comes with some drawbacks:

Learning Curve: LaTeX requires a steeper learning curve compared to word processors. You need to learn the syntax and commands to properly format your documents.

Less Intuitive Interface: LaTeX lacks the graphical user interface of word processors, which some users may find less intuitive.

Limited WYSIWYG Editing: While LaTeX allows for previewing, the editing environment is not entirely WYSIWYG (What You See Is What You Get). This can be frustrating for users accustomed to seeing the final formatted document as they type.

Collaboration Challenges: Collaborating on LaTeX documents can be more challenging than with word processors, especially if not everyone involved is familiar with LaTeX.

1.4 A Brief History of LaTeX

LaTeX was created in 1984 by Leslie Lamport, a computer scientist frustrated with the limitations of existing typesetting systems. He aimed to develop a system that was easier to use than TeX, the underlying typesetting engine, while still producing high-quality output.

Over the years, LaTeX has gained widespread popularity and evolved significantly. Today, it is a mature and powerful system supported by a large and active community.

1.5 Comparison with other document preparation systems

There are several other document preparation systems available, each with its own strengths and weaknesses. Here is a brief comparison of LaTeX with some of the most popular alternatives:

- Microsoft Word: Word is the most widely used word processor, offering a user-friendly interface and extensive features. However, it lacks the precision and control over formatting that LaTeX provides.
- LibreOffice Writer: LibreOffice Writer is a free and open-source alternative to Word offering similar features. However, it also lacks the advanced typesetting capabilities of LaTeX.
- Adobe InDesign: InDesign is a professional desktop publishing application that excels in layout and design. While it provides more control over formatting than Word, it is not as focused on typesetting as LaTeX.

Ultimately, the best document preparation system for you depends on your specific needs and preferences. If you require high-quality typesetting and flexibility, LaTeX is a powerful and valuable tool to consider.

1.6 Summary

This chapter provided an introduction to LaTeX, highlighting its key features, advantages, and disadvantages. We also briefly discussed its history and compared it to other document preparation systems. In the next chapter, we will delve deeper into the world of LaTeX by learning how to set up your environment and start creating your first document.

Chapter 2: Getting Started with LaTeX

Now that you have a basic understanding of what LaTeX is and its benefits, it's time to dive into the practical aspects of getting started. This chapter will guide you through the process of installing and setting up LaTeX, exploring the fundamental structure of a LaTeX document, and finally, compiling and viewing your creation.

2.1 Installing and setting up LaTeX

There are several ways to install and set up LaTeX, depending on your operating system and preferred distribution. Here are some general steps:

1. Choose a distribution: Popular LaTeX distributions include TeX Live (Windows and macOS) and MacTeX (macOS). These distributions include the core LaTeX engine, essential packages, and helpful utilities.

2. Download and install the distribution: Follow the instructions provided by the chosen distribution website to download and install the software.

3. Configure your environment (optional): Some distributions require configuration to ensure your system recognizes LaTeX commands. This may involve setting environment variables or adding paths to your system configuration.

4. Test your installation: Once installed, check if LaTeX is working correctly by opening a terminal and typing the command "latex". If successful, you should see the LaTeX version information displayed.

For detailed installation instructions specific to your operating system and preferred distribution, refer to the official website of the chosen distribution.

2.2 Basic structure of a LaTeX document

A LaTeX document consists of three main parts:

1. Preamble: This section defines the document class, sets options, and loads any necessary packages.

2. Document body: This section contains the actual content of your document, including text, figures, tables, and sections.

3. End matter: This section includes the bibliography, references, and any other supplementary material.

Here is a basic template of a LaTeX document:

```
\documentclass{article} % Defines the document class (article, book,
report, etc.)

\begin{document} % Starts the document body

Your document content goes here...

\end{document} % Ends the document body
```

Within the document body, you will use LaTeX commands to format your text, insert figures and tables, and organize your content into sections.

2.3 Compiling and viewing LaTeX documents

After writing your LaTeX document, you need to compile it to create the final output file. This process involves running the LaTeX command-line program on your document.

Most distributions come with a user-friendly interface for compiling and viewing LaTeX documents. These interfaces often include a text editor, a preview window, and buttons for compiling and viewing the generated document.

Here are some common ways to compile and view LaTeX documents:

- Command line: Open a terminal, navigate to the directory containing your document, and type "pdflatex filename.tex" to compile the document. The output file, typically named "filename.pdf", will be generated in the same directory.
- LaTeX editor: Use a dedicated LaTeX editor like Texmaker or LyX. These editors provide features like syntax highlighting, code completion, and built-in compilation tools for a more convenient editing and viewing experience.

Once you have compiled your document, you can view it using a PDF viewer like Adobe Acrobat Reader.

2.4 Conclusion

Congratulations! You have successfully installed LaTeX, created your first basic document, and learned how to compile and view it. This is just the beginning of your journey with LaTeX. In the following chapters, we will delve deeper into its capabilities, exploring various formatting options, inserting figures and tables, and utilizing powerful features to create professional-looking documents for any purpose.

Chapter 3: Document Structure and Layout

Now that you've mastered the basics of getting started with LaTeX, it's time to explore how to structure and layout your documents effectively. This chapter will guide you through setting document classes and options, defining page layout and margins, formatting sections and subsections, and creating various lists and tables to organize your content efficiently.

3.1 Defining Document Classes and Options

LaTeX offers different document classes for various purposes. The most common ones include:

- article: Used for short papers, reports, and essays.
- book: Designed for longer works like books, theses, and dissertations.
- report: Similar to article but with additional features like a title page and table of contents.
- letter: Used for writing formal letters.

You can specify the document class at the beginning of your document using the `\documentclass` command. For example, to create an article, you would write:

```
\documentclass{article}
```

Additionally, you can customize your document further using options. For instance, the `twoside` option instructs LaTeX to format your document for double-sided printing.

Here are some examples of commonly used options:

- `twoside`: Formats the document for double-sided printing.
- `11pt`: Sets the font size to 11 points.
- `a4paper`: Specifies the paper size to A4.

You can combine multiple options within the `\documentclass` command.

```
\documentclass[twoside,11pt,a4paper]{article}
```

3.2 Setting Page Layout and Margins

LaTeX provides commands to customize page layout and margins according to your preferences. Here are some commands you can use:

- `\textwidth`: Sets the width of the text area.
- `\textheight`: Sets the height of the text area.
- `\topmargin`: Sets the top margin.
- `\oddsidemargin`: Sets the left margin for odd-numbered pages.
- `\evensidemargin`: Sets the left margin for even-numbered pages.

You can define these commands within the document preamble using the `\setlength` command. For example, to set the text width to 6 inches and the top margin to 1 inch:

```
\setlength{\textwidth}{6in}
\setlength{\topmargin}{1in}
```

Remember to adjust these settings according to your specific needs and preferred layout style.

3.3 Formatting Sections and Subsections

LaTeX provides various sectioning commands for organizing your document content. Here are some common sectioning commands:

- `\section`: Defines a major section heading.
- `\subsection`: Defines a subheading within a section.
- `\subsubsection`: Defines a subheading within a subsection.

These commands automatically format the section headings with appropriate font size, spacing, and numbering. For example:

```
\section{Introduction}
This section introduces the topic of this document...

\subsection{Previous Work}
This subsection reviews existing research related to the topic...

\subsubsection{Methodology}
This subsubsection describes the methodology used in the study...
```

LaTeX also provides commands for appendices, references, and other document elements.

3.4 Creating Lists and Tables

LaTeX offers several ways to create lists and tables. Here are some commonly used commands:

- `\begin{itemize}` and `\end{itemize}`: Create unordered lists with bullet points.
- `\begin{enumerate}` and `\end{enumerate}`: Create ordered lists with numbers.
- `\begin{tabular}` and `\end{tabular}`: Create tables with rows and columns.

These commands allow you to customize the format of your lists and tables, including font size, spacing, and alignment. You can also use additional packages like `enumitem` for more advanced list formatting and `tabularx` for flexible table creation.

By utilizing these commands and exploring their various options, you can effectively organize your content and present it in an easily understandable and visually appealing manner.

3.5 Conclusion

In this chapter, we have explored the essential tools for structuring and laying out your LaTeX documents. You learned how to define document classes and options, customize page layout and margins, format sections and subsections, and create lists and tables. By mastering these core concepts, you can build a solid foundation for crafting professional-looking and well-organized documents with LaTeX.

The next chapters will delve deeper into other aspects of LaTeX formatting, including working with text, including figures and tables, and incorporating advanced features to enhance your documents further.

Chapter 4: Working with Text

Now that you've built a solid foundation in document structure and layout, it's time to delve deeper into the world of text formatting in LaTeX. This chapter will equip you with the knowledge and skills to manipulate fonts, styles, paragraphs, quotations, headings, and even incorporate hyperlinks and cross-references, turning your document into an engaging and visually appealing masterpiece.

4.1 Using different fonts and styles

LaTeX allows you to customize the appearance of your text by using various commands for fonts, styles, and highlighting. Here are some commonly used commands:

Fonts:

- `\textbf{...}`: Makes the text bold.
- `\textit{...}`: Makes the text italic.
- `\textsf{...}`: Makes the text sans serif.
- `\texttt{...}`: Makes the text typewriter-style.

Styles:

- `\emph{...}`: Emphasizes the text.
- `\underline{...}`: Underlines the text.
- `\textsc{...}`: Makes the text small caps.

Highlighting:

- `\color{...}{...}`: Colors the text.

- `\usepackage{ulem}` and `\uline{...}`: Underlines the text with a line of a specified color.

Additional packages:

- `\usepackage{fontspec}`: Enables the use of OpenType fonts.
- `\usepackage{xcolor}`: Provides a wider range of colors for highlighting.

By combining these commands, you can create visually diverse and informative text that aligns with the tone and message of your document.

4.2 Formatting paragraphs and quotations

LaTeX offers commands for formatting paragraphs and quotations, ensuring proper indentation, spacing, and visual distinction. Here are some key commands:

Paragraphs:

- `\par`: Starts a new paragraph.
- `\indent`: Indents the first line of a paragraph.
- `\vspace{...}`: Adds vertical space between paragraphs.

Quotations:

- `\begin{quotation}` and `\end{quotation}`: Enclose a block quotation with dedicated indentation.
- `\textit{...}` or `\emph{...}`: Applies italic style to quotations.
- `\usepackage{quotestyle}`: Provides more advanced quotation formatting options.

By utilizing these commands, you can ensure your paragraphs and quotations are visually distinct and contribute to the overall readability and flow of your document.

4.3 Creating headings and subheadings

Headings and subheadings are crucial for organizing your content and guiding your readers through the document. LaTeX provides various commands for creating them with appropriate formatting:

Headings:

- `\section{...}`: Defines a major section heading.
- `\subsection{...}`: Defines a subheading within a section.
- `\subsubsection{...}`: Defines a subheading within a subsection.

Additional commands:

- `\chapter{...}`: Defines a chapter heading (primarily used in books).
- `\appendix`: Starts the appendix section.

These commands automatically format the headings and subheadings with appropriate font size, spacing, and numbering, ensuring a consistent and organized structure throughout your document.

4.4 Adding hyperlinks and cross-references

LaTeX allows you to incorporate hyperlinks and cross-references to enhance navigation and provide additional context for your readers. Here are some key commands:

Hyperlinks:

- `\href{...}{...}`: Creates a hyperlink to a website or document.
- `\usepackage{hyperref}`: Enables hyperlinking within the document itself.

Cross-references:

- `\label{...}`: Adds a label to a specific location in your document.
- `\ref{...}`: References a previously labeled section, figure, or equation.

These commands allow you to link to relevant sections, figures, and resources within your document or even external websites, making it easier for your readers to access further information and navigate the content efficiently.

4.5 Conclusion

By mastering the techniques described in this chapter, you can transform your LaTeX documents into visually appealing and informative text. You learned to utilize fonts, styles, and highlighting to create impactful text, format paragraphs and quotations effectively, and incorporate headings, subheadings, hyperlinks, and cross-references to enhance the clarity and organization of your content. With this knowledge, you are well-equipped to craft professional and engaging documents that resonate with your readers.

The next chapter will delve deeper into the realm of illustrations and data presentation, guiding you through the process of including figures and tables in your LaTeX documents.

Chapter 5: Including Additional Content

Now that you have mastered the art of formatting text in LaTeX, it's time to explore how to incorporate additional content that enriches your document's visual appeal and information delivery. This chapter will guide you through working with images and graphics, creating tables with diverse layouts and styles, adding captions and labels for clarity, and even embedding multimedia content to enhance your readers' experience.

5.1 Working with Images and Graphics

LaTeX allows you to seamlessly integrate images and graphics into your documents. Here are the essential commands:

Including images:

- `\includegraphics{...}`: Includes an image in your document.
- `\usepackage{graphicx}`: Enables image inclusion.
- `\caption{...}`: Adds a caption below the image.
- `\label{...}`: Labels the image for cross-referencing.

Image options:

- `width=...`: Sets the width of the image.
- `height=...`: Sets the height of the image.
- `scale=...`: Scales the image by a specific factor.

Additional packages:

- `\usepackage{subfig}`: Allows subfigures within a single image.

- `\usepackage{wrapfig}`: Wraps text around an image.

Supported image formats:

- PNG, JPG, PDF, EPS, and more

By understanding these commands and options, you can effectively integrate images and graphics into your text, enhancing your document's visual appeal and illustrating your points with visual clarity.

5.2 Creating Tables with Different Layouts and Styles

LaTeX provides powerful tools for creating tables with various layouts and styles, allowing you to present complex data in a clear and organized manner. Here are the key commands:

Creating tables:

- `\begin{tabular}{...}` and `\end{tabular}`: Define the table structure with columns and rows.
- `\multicolumn{...}{...}{...}`: Creates a cell spanning multiple columns.
- `\multirow{...}{...}{...}`: Creates a cell spanning multiple rows.

Table formatting:

- `\hline`: Adds horizontal lines to separate rows.
- `\cline{...}{...}`: Adds horizontal lines to specific cells.
- `\usepackage{booktabs}`: Provides various table formatting styles.
- `\usepackage{array}`: Offers additional options for table customization.

Table alignment:

- `l`: Left alignment.
- `c`: Center alignment.
- `r`: Right alignment.

By mastering these commands and options, you can create tables with different layouts and styles, ensuring your data is presented effectively and readily understandable for your readers.

5.3 Adding Captions and Labels

Adding captions and labels enhances the clarity and organization of your document. Here are the key commands:

Captions:

- `\caption{...}`: Adds a caption to figures and tables.
- `\listoffigures`: Creates a list of all figures.
- `\listoftables`: Creates a list of all tables.

Labels:

- `\label{...}`: Labels a specific location in your document, such as a figure or table.
- `\ref{...}`: Refers to a previously labeled element using its label.

By using these commands, you can provide context for your images and tables, improve navigation within your document, and enhance the overall reader experience.

5.4 Embedding Multimedia Content

LaTeX also allows you to include multimedia content like audio and video files, enriching your document with interactive elements. Here are some methods:

Using multimedia packages:

- `\usepackage{multimedia}`: Enables multimedia playback within the document.
- `\includemedia{...}{...}{...}`: Includes multimedia files with specific dimensions and controls.

External links:

- You can also link to external websites or online multimedia platforms.

Benefits:

- Adding multimedia content can enhance engagement and understanding for your readers.
- It can be particularly useful for presentations, online lectures, and interactive tutorials.

Technical considerations:

- Ensure your chosen multimedia format is compatible with LaTeX and your readers' systems.
- Consider file size and potential accessibility issues.

By exploring these options, you can take your LaTeX documents beyond static text and images, creating a more engaging and interactive experience for your readers.

5.5 Conclusion

In this chapter, you have explored the vast possibilities of including various content types beyond plain text in your LaTeX documents. You learned to incorporate images and graphics, create tables with diverse layouts and styles, add captions and labels for clarity, and even embed multimedia content for an interactive experience. By mastering these techniques, you can enhance your documents' visual appeal, improve data presentation, and provide your readers with a richer and more engaging experience.

Chapter 6: Basic Math Typesetting

Now that you have mastered the fundamentals of document formatting and content inclusion, it's time to delve into the world of math typesetting with LaTeX. This chapter will equip you with the knowledge and tools to effectively express mathematical equations, formulas, and symbols in your documents.

6.1 Inline Math vs. Display Math

LaTeX differentiates between two types of mathematical expressions:

Inline math: Used for expressions that flow within the text, like `<span class="math-inline">x^2 \+ y^2 \= z^2</span>`.

Display math: Used for larger and more complex equations that stand out from the text, like

```
\begin{equation}

E = mc^2

\end{equation}
```

The distinction is crucial for proper formatting and visual clarity.

6.2 Basic Mathematical Operators and Symbols

LaTeX provides a vast library of mathematical operators and symbols readily available for use within your equations. Here are some commonly used examples:

Basic operators:

- `+`: Addition.
- `-`: Subtraction.
- `*`: Multiplication.
- `/`: Division.
- `^`: Exponentiation.
- `_`: Subscript.

Additional operators:

- `\sqrt{...}`: Square root.
- `\log{...}`: Logarithm.
- `\sin{...}`: Sine function.
- `\cos{...}`: Cosine function.
- `\tan{...}`: Tangent function.
- `\sum{...}`: Summation.
- `\int{...}`: Integration.

Symbols:

- `\alpha`: Greek letter alpha.
- `\beta`: Greek letter beta.
- `\pi`: Pi.
- `\infty`: Infinity.
- `\approx`: Approximately equal to.

Explore the comprehensive LaTeX symbol table for a complete list and further details.

6.3 Fractions, Exponents, and Radicals

LaTeX offers specific commands for formatting fractions, exponents, and radicals:

Fractions:

- `\frac{...}{...}`: Creates a fraction with numerator and denominator.
- `\tfrac{...}{...}`: Creates a smaller fraction.

Exponents:

- `x^n`: Raises x to the power of n.
- `\exp{...}`: Exponential function.

Radicals:

- `\sqrt{...}`: Square root.
- `\sqrt[n]{...}`: nth root.
- `\∛{...}`: Cube root.

By mastering these commands, you can format your fractions, exponents, and radicals with precision and clarity.

6.4 Matrices and Equations

LaTeX provides powerful tools for creating and formatting matrices and equations:

Matrices:

- `\begin{matrix}` and `\end{matrix}`: Define a matrix.
- `&`: Separates columns within a row.

- `\\`: Separates rows.
- `\usepackage{amsmath}`: Enables advanced matrix features.

Equations:

- `\begin{equation}` and `\end{equation}`: Define a single equation.
- `\begin{align*}` and `\end{align*}`: Define multiple aligned equations.
- `\label{...}`: Labels an equation for referencing.

By understanding these commands, you can effectively express complex mathematical relationships and calculations in your LaTeX documents.

6.5 Conclusion

This chapter provided you with a solid foundation in basic math typesetting with LaTeX. You learned to distinguish between inline and display math, utilize various mathematical operators and symbols, format fractions, exponents, and radicals, and create matrices and equations. With these tools at your disposal, you can now confidently express your mathematical ideas and calculations in your LaTeX documents with clarity and precision.

The next chapter will delve deeper into advanced math typesetting techniques, exploring additional features and packages to further enhance your mathematical expressions and equations.

Chapter 7: Advanced Math Typesetting

Building upon your foundational knowledge of basic math typesetting with LaTeX, this chapter delves deeper into advanced techniques for expressing complex mathematical concepts with precision and clarity. You will learn methods for aligning equations and multi-line expressions, explore specialized mathematical fonts and symbols, discover how to create custom math environments, and master the art of referencing and numbering equations for efficient communication and navigation.

7.1 Aligning Equations and Multi-Line Expressions

LaTeX provides various tools for aligning equations and multi-line expressions, ensuring a visually consistent and organized presentation of your mathematical content. Here are some key methods:

Aligned Equations:

- `\begin{align*}...\end{align*}`: Aligns equations at specific points (e.g., equal signs).
- `&`: Defines the alignment point within an equation.
- `\\`: Separates lines within an equation.
- `\usepackage{amsmath}`: Enables additional alignment features like `\begin{align}` for numbered equations.

Multi-Line Expressions:

- `\begin{array}{c}...\end{array}`: Creates a multi-line expression with centered alignment.

- `\renewcommand{\arraystretch}{1.5}`: Adjusts the vertical spacing between lines.
- `\usepackage{amsmath}`: Enables advanced options like `\substack` for stacking expressions.

By utilizing these tools effectively, you can enhance the visual clarity and readability of your complex mathematical expressions and equations.

7.2 Using Mathematical Fonts and Symbols

LaTeX offers various mathematical fonts and symbols to express specific concepts and enhance the visual appeal of your equations. Here are some notable examples:

Mathematical Fonts:

- `\mathcal{...}`: Calligraphic font for sets and functions.
- `\mathfrak{...}`: Fraktur font for Lie algebras.
- `\mathbb{...}`: Blackboard bold for number sets.

Specialized Symbols:

- `\nabla`: Gradient operator.
- `\partial`: Partial derivative.
- `\in`: Element of.
- `\subset`: Subset of.
- `\infty`: Infinity symbol.

These fonts and symbols are readily available within the LaTeX environment. Additionally, dedicated packages like `amssymb` and `amsmath` provide an even broader range of specialized options.

7.3 Creating Custom Math Environments

LaTeX allows you to define custom math environments for specific types of equations or expressions frequently used in your work. This promotes consistency and efficiency within your document. Here's how:

- `\newenvironment{myenv}{...}{...}`: Defines a new environment named `myenv` with opening and closing commands.
- `\begin{myenv}`: Starts the custom environment.
- `\end{myenv}`: Ends the custom environment.

Within the environment, you can specify desired formatting, alignment, and spacing using LaTeX commands. This allows you to create reusable templates for specific mathematical expressions, streamlining your workflow.

7.4 Referencing and Numbering Equations

Referencing and numbering equations are crucial for efficient navigation within your document and ensuring clear communication of mathematical relationships. Here's how to achieve this:

Numbering Equations:

- `\begin{equation}` and `\end{equation}`: Number equations automatically within the document.
- `\label{eq:mylabel}`: Adds a unique label to an equation for referencing.

Referencing Equations:

- `\ref{eq:mylabel}`: References the equation labeled with `eq:mylabel`.

By utilizing these techniques, you can easily link equations to relevant sections of your text and guide your readers through complex mathematical concepts with clarity and precision.

7.5 Conclusion

This chapter has equipped you with advanced tools and techniques for mastering math typesetting in LaTeX. You explored methods for aligning equations and multi-line expressions, discovered specialized mathematical fonts and symbols, learned to create custom math environments, and mastered referencing and numbering equations. By effectively applying these techniques, you can now express complex mathematical concepts in your LaTeX documents with enhanced clarity, visual appeal, and efficient navigation for your readers.

The next chapter will broaden your horizons by exploring additional tools and packages for further customization and advanced features in LaTeX.

Chapter 8: Compiling and Building Documents

Once you have crafted your LaTeX document with text, formatting, and content, it's time to compile it into a finished product. This chapter will guide you through the process of using different LaTeX compilers, batch compiling multiple files, and troubleshooting common compilation errors, equipping you with the skills to efficiently build your documents and ensure a smooth workflow.

8.1 Using Different LaTeX Compilers

LaTeX relies on various compilers to process your code and generate the final output. Here are some commonly used compilers:

- pdflatex: Converts your LaTeX code into a PDF document, the most common format for sharing and viewing.
- latex: Compiles the LaTeX code into an intermediate format (.dvi) for further processing.
- xelatex: Supports compiling documents with fonts beyond the standard LaTeX repertoire, including OpenType fonts.
- lualatex: Similar to xelatex but with additional features like bidirectional text support.

The choice of compiler depends on your specific needs and desired output format. Most LaTeX distributions include these compilers by default.

8.2 Batch Compiling Multiple Files

Your LaTeX project might involve multiple files, such as the main document, figures, and bibliography. Compiling each file individually can be cumbersome. Thankfully,

LaTeX allows for batch compiling, which processes all relevant files automatically. Here are two common methods:

- Command line: Navigate to the directory containing your main LaTeX file and use the following command:

```
pdflatex *.tex
```

This command will compile all `.tex` files within the directory.

- LaTeX editors: Most editors offer built-in batch compiling functionality, allowing you to compile the entire project with a single click.

Batch compiling streamlines your workflow and ensures all files are compiled consistently, saving you time and effort.

8.3 Troubleshooting Common Compilation Errors

Unfortunately, errors are inevitable during the compilation process. However, understanding and troubleshooting these errors is crucial for successfully building your documents. Here are some common errors and tips for resolving them:

- Missing files: Ensure all referenced files like figures and bibliographies are present in the correct directory.
- Syntax errors: Carefully review your LaTeX code for typos, missing punctuation, or incorrect commands.
- Package issues: Verify that all required packages are installed and properly configured.

- Undefined references: Check if all citations and references are properly defined and labeled.

Many online resources provide detailed explanations and solutions for specific compilation errors. Additionally, most LaTeX editors offer built-in error detection and highlighting features to help you identify and fix them efficiently.

8.4 Conclusion

By understanding the different LaTeX compilers, mastering batch compiling techniques, and acquiring troubleshooting skills, you can confidently navigate the compilation process and ensure your LaTeX documents are built seamlessly and error-free. This allows you to focus on creating high-quality content and sharing your ideas with the world in a polished and professional format.

The next chapter will delve into the fascinating world of advanced LaTeX features, introducing you to tools and techniques for further customization and automation, empowering you to craft even more sophisticated and impactful documents.

Chapter 9: Managing Bibliography and References

Effectively managing your bibliography and references is crucial for any research paper, academic report, or document containing citations. This chapter will equip you with the knowledge and tools to create and manage your bibliography files, seamlessly insert citations and references within your text, and utilize reference management software to streamline your workflow.

9.1 Creating and Managing Bibliography Files

LaTeX relies on separate `.bib` files to store bibliographic information. Here's how to manage them:

Creating a bibliography file:

- Open a text editor (e.g., Notepad, TextEdit).
- Add entries using specific BibTeX syntax for each reference.
- Include details like author, title, publication date, etc.
- Save the file with a `.bib` extension.

Managing bibliography files:

- Use a dedicated bibliography editor for easier entry management.
- Organize entries with keywords and tags for efficient searching.
- Utilize BibTeX utilities for automated sorting and formatting.

Keeping your bibliography file organized and well-maintained ensures consistency and accuracy in referencing throughout your document.

9.2 Inserting Citations and References in the Text

LaTeX provides commands for inserting citations and references within your text:

- `\cite{...}`: Inserts a citation within the text, referencing a specific entry in your `.bib` file.
- `\bibliography{...}`: Defines the location of your `.bib` file for bibliography generation.
- `\bibliographystyle{...}`: Specifies the formatting style for your bibliography entries.

By understanding these commands and utilizing proper syntax, you can seamlessly integrate references into your text, ensuring clear and accurate attribution of sources.

9.3 Using Reference Management Software

Reference management software offers powerful tools for managing your bibliography and keeping your references organized. Here are some benefits:

- Automated bibliography generation: Import references from various sources and automatically generate a formatted bibliography.
- Citation insertion: Easily insert citations into your text with the software's built-in features.
- Duplicate detection: Identify and avoid duplicate entries in your bibliography.
- Collaboration features: Share your bibliography and collaborate with others on research projects.

Popular reference management software includes Mendeley, Zotero, and EndNote. These tools can significantly enhance your research workflow and ensure efficient and accurate reference management.

9.4 Conclusion

Mastering the techniques presented in this chapter empowers you to effectively manage your bibliography and references in LaTeX documents. You learned to create and manage `.bib` files, insert citations and references seamlessly, and leverage the power of reference management software. By utilizing these tools and techniques, you can ensure accurate and consistent referencing, enhance the credibility and professionalism of your documents, and streamline your research workflow.

The next chapter will delve into the realm of customization and automation, introducing you to advanced LaTeX features like macros, templates, and packages, allowing you to create even more sophisticated and personalized documents.

Chapter 10: Using Packages and Extensions

While the core LaTeX functionality is powerful, it can be further enhanced through packages and extensions. This chapter will introduce you to the world of package management, explore popular packages for specific tasks, and provide guidance on creating custom packages to personalize your LaTeX workflow.

10.1 Installing and Using LaTeX Packages

Packages provide additional features and functionality to your LaTeX environment. Here's how to utilize them:

Installation:

- Use your LaTeX distribution's package manager (e.g., `tlmgr`, `apt-get`) to install packages.
- Download and install packages manually from trusted online repositories.

Usage:

- Include the package command (`\usepackage{...}`) in your preamble to activate its features.
- Refer to the package documentation for specific commands and options.

Popular package repositories include CTAN (Comprehensive TeX Archive Network) and MiKTeX. Explore these repositories to discover a vast array of packages catering to diverse needs and functionalities.

10.2 Popular Packages for Specific Tasks

Here's a glimpse into some popular packages for specific tasks:

Document formatting:

- `amsmath`: Advanced math typesetting.
- `graphicx`: Image inclusion.
- `tabularx`: Flexible table creation.

Bibliography management:

- `biblatex`: Extended bibliography formatting options.
- `natbib`: Citation management with author-year style.

Other popular packages:

- `hyperref`: Hyperlinks and cross-references.
- `algorithm`: Algorithm typesetting.
- `color`: Text and background color customization.

This is just a small selection of the vast collection of available packages. Explore online resources and communities to discover packages tailored to your specific needs and enhance your LaTeX workflow.

10.3 Creating Custom Packages

For advanced users, creating custom packages provides a powerful tool for personalizing LaTeX. Here's an overview of the process:

- Define the package structure using `\ProvidesPackage{...}` and `\RequirePackage{...}`.

- Create new commands and macros using `\newcommand{...}` and `\newenvironment{...}`.
- Implement functionalities specific to your desired tasks.
- Document your package for clear usage and understanding.

Creating custom packages requires knowledge of LaTeX internals and programming concepts. However, it offers a significant level of control and customization, allowing you to tailor LaTeX to your unique workflow and needs.

10.4 Conclusion

By embracing the world of LaTeX packages and extensions, you can significantly expand the capabilities of your LaTeX environment. You learned how to install and use packages, discovered popular packages for specific tasks, and gained insights into creating custom packages. This knowledge empowers you to personalize your workflow, enhance the functionality of your documents, and achieve professional-looking results.

The next chapter will explore advanced topics in LaTeX, delving into concepts like document automation, scripting, and integration with external tools, taking your LaTeX skills to the next level.

Chapter 11: Automating Repetitive Tasks

As you create more and more LaTeX documents, you may find yourself repeating the same tasks over and over again. This chapter will equip you with the skills to automate repetitive tasks using macros, templates, and scripts, saving you time and effort while ensuring consistency and quality across your documents.

11.1 Writing and Using Macros

Macros allow you to define shortcuts for frequently used text or commands. Here's how:

- Use the `\newcommand{...}` command.
- Define the macro name, arguments (optional), and replacement text.
- Use the macro name within your document to replace the defined text.

For example:

```
\newcommand{\mycommand}[1]{\textbf{#1}}
```

```
My document contains \mycommand{important information}.
```

This will replace `\mycommand{important information}` with "important information" throughout your document.

Macros promote efficiency and consistency, especially for complex commands or frequently used text snippets.

11.2 Creating Templates and Document Styles

Templates provide a pre-defined structure and formatting for your documents, saving you time setting up repetitive elements. Here's how to create and use them:

- Create a basic LaTeX document with your desired structure and formatting.
- Save the file as a `.tex` template.
- Use the `\input{...}` command to include the template in your new documents.

You can also create custom document styles using packages like `fancyhdr` for headers and footers or `titlesec` for section formatting. These styles ensure consistency and professionalism across your documents.

11.3 Automating Common Tasks with Scripts

Scripts offer a powerful way to automate complex and repetitive tasks in LaTeX. Here's how:

- Use scripting languages like Lua or Python.
- Integrate the scripts with your LaTeX workflow with tools like `lualatex` or `pdflatex`.
- Automate tasks like file conversion, batch processing, and generating customized content.

While scripting requires more advanced knowledge, it can significantly enhance your efficiency and automate complex workflows, saving you time and effort while achieving consistent and high-quality results.

11.4 Conclusion

By mastering the techniques presented in this chapter, you can automate repetitive tasks in LaTeX, significantly enhancing your productivity and workflow efficiency. You learned to write and use macros, create templates and document styles, and even automate complex tasks with scripts. These skills empower you to streamline your LaTeX workflow, produce professional-looking documents consistently, and dedicate more time to the creative aspects of your work.

The final chapter will explore advanced LaTeX topics, delving into integration with other software, exploring the LaTeX community, and providing insights into the future of LaTeX. This comprehensive guide will equip you with the knowledge and skills to become a proficient and confident LaTeX user.

Chapter 12: The Power of LaTeX

This final chapter serves as a culmination of your LaTeX journey, reflecting on the key features and benefits you've encountered, providing resources for further learning, and offering valuable tips and tricks to become a LaTeX pro.

12.1 Recap of Key Features and Benefits

Let's recap the key features and benefits that make LaTeX such a powerful tool:

Professional-looking documents: LaTeX produces high-quality typesetting, ideal for academic papers, books, reports, and other professional documents.

Flexibility and customization: LaTeX provides extensive control over every aspect of your document layout and formatting, allowing for tailored and personalized outputs.

Version control and collaboration: LaTeX promotes collaboration through version control using tools like Git and Subversion, ensuring seamless integration with team projects.

Rich ecosystem of packages: A vast array of packages cater to specific needs and functionalities, expanding LaTeX's capabilities to address virtually any typesetting challenge.

Open-source and free: LaTeX is free to use and open-source, fostering a vibrant community and continuous development, ensuring long-term support and accessibility.

By mastering these features, you can leverage the power of LaTeX to create visually appealing, professionally formatted, and highly accurate documents, enhancing your communication and presentation across various domains.

12.2 Resources for Further Learning

Your journey with LaTeX is far from over. Here are some resources to continue your learning and exploration:

Online documentation: The official LaTeX Project website provides comprehensive documentation and tutorials: https://www.latex-project.org/help/documentation/.

CTAN (Comprehensive TeX Archive Network): An extensive repository of LaTeX packages, macros, templates, and other resources: https://ctan.org/?lang=en.

Books and tutorials: Numerous books and online tutorials cater to different learning styles and areas of focus.

LaTeX communities and forums: Participating in online communities and forums allows you to connect with other LaTeX users for support, discussion, and sharing knowledge.

Online courses and workshops: Dedicated online courses and workshops offer structured learning paths for enhancing your LaTeX skills.

By actively engaging with these resources, you can continue to expand your knowledge, explore new capabilities, and refine your LaTeX skills to a professional level.

12.3 Tips and Tricks for Becoming a LaTeX Pro

Here are some valuable tips and tricks to become a LaTeX pro:

Start with the basics: Master the fundamental concepts of LaTeX syntax and commands before venturing into advanced features.

Practice consistently: Regular practice is key to solidifying your understanding and developing strong LaTeX skills.

Utilize templates and styles: Leverage pre-defined templates and styles to save time and ensure consistent formatting.

Explore new packages: Discover and experiment with new packages to expand your capabilities and address specific needs.

Join the community: Actively participate in online communities and forums to learn from others and contribute to the LaTeX ecosystem.

Share your knowledge: Share your LaTeX expertise by creating tutorials, answering questions, and contributing to open-source projects.

Never stop learning: LaTeX is constantly evolving, so stay informed about updates, new features, and best practices.

By embracing these tips and tricks, you can embark on a rewarding journey of mastering LaTeX and become a proficient user, capable of creating high-quality, professional documents that effectively communicate your ideas and impress your audience.

12.4 Conclusion

Throughout this book, you have explored the fascinating world of LaTeX, learning its features, functionalities, and applications. You have acquired the knowledge and skills to create professional-looking documents, enhance your workflow through automation, and delve into advanced topics. Remember, the journey with LaTeX is a continuous learning process. Embrace the challenges, explore new possibilities, and contribute to the vibrant community. By doing so, you can unlock the full potential of LaTeX and become a true master of this powerful tool.

Appendices

Appendix A: Quick Reference Guide

This appendix provides a comprehensive list of common LaTeX commands and symbols for quick reference.

General Commands:

- `\documentclass{...}`: Specifies the document class (e.g., article, book, report).
- `\usepackage{...}`: Loads additional packages for specific functionalities.
- `\begin{document}`: Starts the document body.
- `\end{document}`: Ends the document body.
- `\section{...}`: Creates a section heading.
- `\subsection{...}`: Creates a subsection heading.
- `\subsubsection{...}`: Creates a subsubsection heading.
- `\\`: Inserts a line break.
- `\hspace{...}`: Adds horizontal space.
- `\vspace{...}`: Adds vertical space.
- `\noindent`: Aligns text to the left margin without indentation.

Text Formatting:

- `\textbf{...}`: Makes text bold.
- `\textit{...}`: Makes text italic.
- `\underline{...}`: Underlines text.
- `\emph{...}`: Emphasizes text.
- `\textsf{...}`: Makes text sans-serif.
- `\texttt{...}`: Makes text typewriter style.

Lists:

- `\begin{enumerate}` and `\end{enumerate}`: Create a numbered list.
- `\begin{itemize}` and `\end{itemize}`: Create an unnumbered list.
- `\item`: Defines an item in a list.

Tables:

- `\begin{tabular}{...}` and `\end{tabular}`: Defines a table structure.
- `|`: Separates columns within a row.
- `\\`: Separates rows within a table.

Math Symbols:

- `+`: Addition.
- `-`: Subtraction.
- `*`: Multiplication.
- `/`: Division.
- `^`: Exponentiation.
- `_`: Subscript.
- `\sqrt{...}`: Square root.
- `\pi`: Pi.
- `\infty`: Infinity.
- `\approx`: Approximately equal to.

Additional Resources:

- CTAN: https://ctan.org/?lang=en
- The LaTeX Project: https://www.latex-project.org/

- Wikibooks LaTeX Tutorial:
  https://upload.wikimedia.org/wikipedia/commons/2/2d/LaTeX.pdf

Note: This list is not exhaustive. Please refer to the official LaTeX documentation and online resources for a complete list of commands and symbols.

Appendix B: Easy Access to Frequently Used Features

This appendix provides quick and easy access to frequently used features in LaTeX, categorized for your convenience.

1. Document Formatting:

- Font sizes:
    - `\tiny`: Very small font.
    - `\scriptsize`: Smaller font.
    - `\footnotesize`: Small font.
    - `\normalsize`: Standard font size.
    - `\large`: Large font.
    - `\Large`: Larger font.
    - `\LARGE`: Very large font.
-
- Text alignment:
    - `\flushleft`: Align text to the left margin.
    - `\flushright`: Align text to the right margin.
    - `\center`: Center text.
-
- Indentation and spacing:
    - `\noindent`: No indentation.
    - `\indent`: Indent the first line of a paragraph.
    - `\hspace{...}`: Add horizontal space.
    - `\vspace{...}`: Add vertical space.
-
- Line breaks:
    - `\\`: Line break.

- ○ `\pagebreak`: Page break.
-

2. Mathematical Expressions:

- Basic operators:
  - ○ `+`: Addition.
  - ○ `-`: Subtraction.
  - ○ `*`: Multiplication.
  - ○ `/`: Division.
  - ○ `^`: Exponentiation.
  - ○ `_`: Subscript.
  - ○ `\bar{...}`: Overline.
  - ○ `\hat{...}`: Hat.
-
- Fractions:
  - ○ `\frac{...}{...}`: Fraction with numerator and denominator.
  - ○ `\tfrac{...}{...}`: Smaller fraction.
-
- Radicals:
  - ○ `\sqrt{...}`: Square root.
  - ○ `\sqrt[n]{...}`: nth root.
  - ○ `\∛{...}`: Cube root.
-
- Sums and integrals:
  - ○ `\sum{...}`: Summation.
  - ○ `\int{...}`: Integration.
-
- Matrices:

- ○ `\begin{pmatrix}` and `\end{pmatrix}`: Parentheses matrix.
- ○ `\begin{bmatrix}` and `\end{bmatrix}`: Brackets matrix.
- ○ `\begin{vmatrix}` and `\end{vmatrix}`: Vertical bars matrix.
- ○ `\begin{array}{c|ccc}`: Custom matrix with alignment.

.

3. References and Citations:

- `\cite{...}`: Insert citation within the text.
- `\bibliography{...}`: Define the location of the bibliography file.
- `\bibliographystyle{...}`: Specify the formatting style for bibliography entries.

4. Package Usage:

- `\usepackage{...}`: Include additional packages for specific functionalities.
- `\usepackage[options]{...}`: Include a package with specific options.

5. Useful Commands:

- `\today`: Print today's date.
- `\newpage`: Start a new page.
- `\hphantom{...}`: Placeholder for horizontal space.
- `\vphantom{...}`: Placeholder for vertical space.
- `\mbox{...}`: Create a box around text.

This appendix provides a brief overview of frequently used features in LaTeX. Please refer to the official LaTeX documentation and online resources for a more comprehensive understanding and additional features.

Appendix C: Essential LaTeX Terminology

This appendix provides definitions of essential LaTeX terminology to enhance your understanding of the language and its functionalities.

1. Basic Terminology:

- Document class: A template that defines the overall structure and format of your document, such as `article`, `book`, or `report`.
- Package: A collection of commands and macros that provide additional functionalities beyond the core LaTeX commands.
- Command: A keyword in LaTeX that performs a specific action, such as `\documentclass` or `\begin{document}`.
- Macro: A shortcut that defines a reusable command for complex tasks or frequently used text.
- Environment: A block of text that uses specific commands to set the formatting and behavior of its contents, such as `\begin{enumerate}` for a list or `\begin{equation}` for an equation.
- Argument: A value provided to a command or macro to specify its behavior, such as the text to be formatted or the number of columns in a table.
- Option: A modifier that changes the default behavior of a command or package, such as the font size or the spacing between lines.

2. Mathematical Terminology:

- Delimiters: Symbols used to enclose mathematical expressions, such as parentheses, brackets, and braces.
- Superscript: A character written above and slightly smaller than the main line, often used for exponents.

- Subscript: A character written below and slightly smaller than the main line, often used for indexes.
- Operator: A symbol that represents a mathematical operation, such as addition, subtraction, or multiplication.
- Function: A mathematical expression that maps one set of values to another, often denoted by a letter or symbol.
- Matrix: A rectangular array of numbers or other values arranged in rows and columns.
- Equation: A mathematical statement that expresses two quantities as equal.
- Inequality: A mathematical statement that expresses two quantities as not equal.

3. Reference and Citation Terminology:

- Bibliography: A list of references cited in the body of your document, typically formatted according to a specific style.
- Citation: A reference to a source of information within the text of your document, usually indicated by a number or author's name.
- Citation style: A set of guidelines for formatting citations and references in your document, such as APA, MLA, or Chicago.
- Bibliographic database: A software program used to store and manage bibliographic information.
- Citation management software: A software program used to insert citations and generate bibliographies in your document.

4. Additional Terminology:

- Compile: To convert your LaTeX code into a finished document, such as a PDF or DVI file.

- Log file: A file that records any errors or warnings encountered during the compilation process.
- Auxiliary files: Files generated during the compilation process that are necessary to create the final document.
- Template: A pre-formatted document that can be used as a starting point for your own documents.
- Previewer: A program that allows you to view your LaTeX document as it will appear when printed or converted to PDF.

Understanding these essential terms will significantly enhance your understanding of LaTeX and its capabilities. By familiarizing yourself with this vocabulary, you can navigate the LaTeX documentation and online resources more confidently, expanding your knowledge and skills in this powerful typesetting tool.

Appendix D: Online Resources

This appendix provides a comprehensive list of online resources for LaTeX users, offering support, tutorials, communities, and various tools to enhance your LaTeX experience.

Websites:

- The LaTeX Project: https://www.latex-project.org/
  - Official website of the LaTeX Project, including documentation, news, and resources.
- CTAN (Comprehensive TeX Archive Network): https://ctan.org/?lang=en
  - Largest repository of LaTeX packages, macros, templates, and other resources.
- Overleaf: https://www.overleaf.com/
  - Online LaTeX editor with collaboration features and a user-friendly interface.
- ShareLaTeX: https://www.sharelatex.com/
  - Another online LaTeX editor with version control and real-time collaboration.
- TeX Users Group (TUG): https://tug.org/
  - Non-profit organization promoting the use of TeX and LaTeX.

Tutorials:

- The LaTeX Tutorial: https://latex-tutorial.com/
  - Comprehensive online tutorial covering all aspects of LaTeX.
- Wikibooks LaTeX Tutorial:
  https://upload.wikimedia.org/wikipedia/commons/2/2d/LaTeX.pdf

- ○ Extensive and detailed LaTeX tutorial in PDF format.
- Learn LaTeX in 30 Minutes:

  https://www.overleaf.com/learn/latex/Learn_LaTeX_in_30_minutes
  - ○ Quick and easy introduction to LaTeX for beginners.
- MIT OpenCourseware Introduction to LaTeX:

  https://ocw.mit.edu/courses/18-310-principles-of-discrete-applied-mathematics-fall-2013/5e1a98e4bc4a1bc1965a17a9b63ffed8_MIT18_310F13_intro.pdf
  - ○ Free online course from MIT covering the fundamentals of LaTeX.
-

Communities:

- TeX Stack Exchange: https://tex.stackexchange.com/
  - ○ Q&A platform for LaTeX users to ask and answer questions.
-
- LaTeX subreddit: https://www.reddit.com/r/LaTeX/
  - ○ subreddit dedicated to LaTeX discussions, news, and resources.
-
- LaTeX forums: https://latex.org/forum/
  - ○ Online forum for LaTeX users to discuss various topics and seek help.
-

Other Resources:

- LaTeX templates: https://www.sharelatex.com/
  - ○ Collection of ready-made LaTeX templates for different document types.
- LaTeX packages: https://ctan.org/pkg/classes?lang=en

- ○ Extensive directory of LaTeX packages for various functionalities.
- ●
- ● LaTeX editors: https://www.overleaf.com/
  - ○ Comparison of different LaTeX editors for various platforms.
- ●

Additional Support:

- Many universities and libraries offer LaTeX workshops and training sessions.
- Online and offline books can provide in-depth tutorials and reference guides.
- Consider using professional LaTeX services for complex documents or specialized needs.

By exploring these online resources, you can access valuable support, tutorials, communities, and tools to enhance your LaTeX skills and create professional-looking documents with confidence.

www.ingramcontent.com/pod-product-compliance
Lightning Source LLC
LaVergne TN
LVHW051618050326
832903LV00033B/4560